Kids in Their Communities™

I Live in the Mountains

Stasia Ward Kehoe

The Rosen Publishing Group's

PowerKids Press™

New York

For Kevin, Thomas, and Mak

Published in 2000 by The Rosen Publishing Group, Inc.
29 East 21st Street, New York, NY 10010

First Edition

Book Design: Michael de Guzman

Photo Credits and Photo Illustrations: pp. 4, 8, 11, 12, 15, 16 by Michelle Davis; pp. 7, 20 Courtesy of Colorado Springs Convention and Visitors Bureau; p. 19 CORBIS/David Muench.

Kehoe, Stasia Ward, 1968–
        I live in the mountains / Stasia Ward Kehoe.
                p. cm. — (Kids in their communities)
        Includes index.
Summary: A ten-year-old girl who lives in the mountains of Colorado describes her life in that rural community including views from her home in the woods and weekly drives to nearby cities.
        ISBN 0-8239-5442-0
    1. Florissant Region (Colo.)—Social life and customs Juvenile literature. 2. Mountain life—Colorado—Florissant Region Juvenile literature. 3. City and town life—Colorado—Florissant Juvenile literature. 4. Children—Colorado—Florissant Region—Social life and customs Juvenile literature. [1. Mountain life—Colorado. 2. City and town life—Colorado. 3. Colorado—Social life and customs.] I. Title. II. Series: Kehoe, Stasia Ward, 1968– Kids in their communities.
F784.F53K44   2000   99-26371
978.8'58—dc21   CIP

Manufactured in the United States of America

CONTENTS

Charissa

My name is Charissa. I am 10 years old. My family and I live in the mountains of Colorado. Colorado is the highest state in America. Every part of our state is over 3,000 feet above sea level. Sea level means the level of the **surface** of the sea. You can describe how high a place is, or how tall a mountain is, by saying how far it is above sea level.

Sometimes I enjoy Colorado's fresh mountain air by playing on my tire swing.

The Rocky Mountains

My town, Florissant, is just a few miles from Pike's Peak, one of the most famous peaks in the Rocky Mountain Range. The Rocky Mountains, or Rockies, run all the way from New Mexico to Canada. The Rockies are part of the Continental Divide. This means that rivers to the east of the Rockies run east toward the Atlantic or Arctic Oceans. Rivers to the west of the Rockies run west toward the Pacific Ocean.

Lots of visitors come to Colorado to see Pike's Peak. ▶

6

At Home in the Woods

My house is almost 10,000 feet above sea level. We have a porch all the way around our house, so you can sit outside and look at the view. No matter which direction I look, I can see beautiful trees and mountains. I don't see many houses. Not many families live this far up in the mountains. We do have lots of animal neighbors, though. Bears, mountain lions, beaver, elk, deer, porcupines, and foxes live in the woods near my house.

◀ *From my porch, I can look at all the beautiful mountains.*

Power and Water

On top of our roof is a television satellite dish. I live so far up in the mountains that there is no cable television. No one comes to deliver the mail or pick up the garbage. Our mail is delivered to a post office box in town. Each week my mom or dad loads up the garbage into the car and takes it to the dump. Our water comes from a well dug in our front yard. The well is 400 feet deep!

We need a television satellite dish to get some programs on television because cable companies don't work up here.

School

My school looks a lot like my house. That is because it is my house! I am **home-schooled**. Mom teaches me, my sister, and my brothers right in our house. Once or twice a year, Mom brings us to Denver, the capital of Colorado. She talks to people in the **legislature** about how things are going with our home schooling. Mom was one of the people who worked hard to pass the home-schooling law in the state of Colorado.

◀ *I think it is neat to go to school in my own house!*

Kit Carson

We study the same things at home that other kids study at school. Right now, I am studying cursive writing, math, and reading. I like history, too. It is fun to learn about the pioneers who lived in Colorado many years ago. Pioneers are the first people to explore a new place. One of my favorite pioneers is Kit Carson, who helped to guide **explorers** through Colorado and all the way to California. In the 1840s, Kit Carson had a cabin not far from where my house is today.

Kit Carson's cabin is still standing. It has just one room with a bed, table, chairs, and a wood-burning stove.

Flowers in Florissant

My family belongs to the Florissant Heritage Foundation. This is a group that works hard to take care of the old **ranches** and other buildings that are important to our town's history. The group also helps to keep Florissant beautiful. Lots of people pass through our town on their way to ski or hike in the mountains. We want our town to look nice for visitors and for the people who live here. In the summer, we decorate the town with **barrels** of flowers.

◄ *My brother helps water the flowers so they will be beautiful all summer long.*

Florissant Fossils

One of the neatest places to visit in my town is the Florissant Fossil Beds National Monument. When you go there, you can see fossils of insects, seeds, and leaves. There are also huge **petrified sequoia** tree stumps that have turned into stone over thousands of years. Visiting the fossil beds is like taking a trip back in time. You can learn what the land in my town looked like in **prehistoric** times. It's neat to see fossils of all the plants, trees, and bugs that lived in Florissant way before me!

This petrified tree stump at the Florissant Fossil Beds is thousands of years old. ▶

Colorado Springs

About once a week, we drive down to the city of Colorado Springs. It is 40 miles away from Florissant. Sometimes in the winter, the roads are too icy and dangerous to make the trip. In 1997, we had a **blizzard** that lasted three days. Four feet of snow fell on the ground. That's almost as tall as me! That winter, we did not get to Colorado Springs for a long time.

◀ *Here is a look at downtown Colorado Springs.*

Mountain Life

The tops of the Rocky Mountains are covered with snow all year long, not just in the winter. My favorite times of year are spring and summer. That's when the lower parts of the mountains are covered with wildflowers. I like living in the mountains because I can be close to nature all the time. I hope that I will always live in such a beautiful place!

Glossary

barrels (BAYR-ulz) Containers with a flat top and bottom and curved sides.

blizzard (BLIH-zurd) A bad snowstorm with very strong winds.

explorers (ik-SPLOR-urz) People who travel to different places to learn more about them.

home-schooled (HOME-skoold) To be taught at home instead of at school.

legislature (LEH-juh-slay-chur) A group of people that have the power to make the laws of a state or country.

petrified (PEH-trih-fyd) When something, such as wood, has turned to stone over thousands of years.

prehistoric (proe-his-TOR-ik) The time before written history.

ranches (RAN-chiz) Large farms for raising horses, beef cattle, or sheep.

sequoia (sih-COY-uh) A cone-bearing evergreen tree that can grow to over 300 feet tall.

surface (SUR-fiss) The top or outside of something.

Index

Web Sites:

Check out this Web site:
http://www.colorado.com/

24